Table of Contents

Traits

No other person looks or acts just like you. You might have brown eyes like your brother. You might run fast like your mother. But you are different from them in other ways.

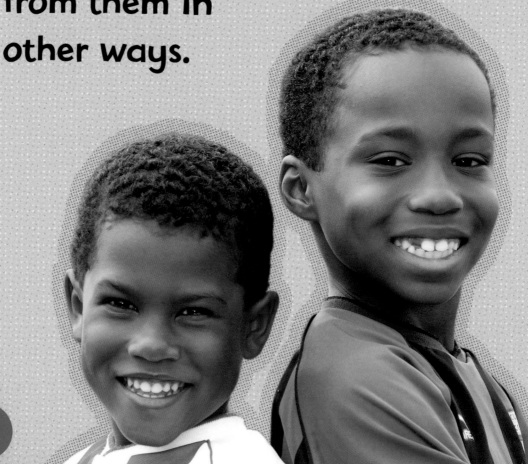

The ways in which people differ are called traits. Skin color is one trait. Freckles are another. People have many traits.

This girl has dimples. Her friend does not. Dimples are a trait.

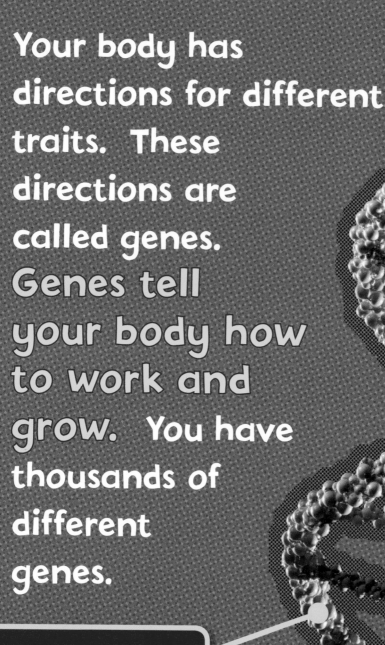

Your body has directions for different traits. These directions are called genes. Genes tell your body how to work and grow. You have thousands of different genes.

This picture of a gene was made on a computer.

Genes come in pairs. You got your genes from your birth parents. One copy of each gene came from your mom. The other copy came from your dad.

Birth parents are related to their kids. Adoptive parents take a child into their family and become his or her parents.

People are more alike than different. They share most of the same traits. You are more like other people than you are like a dog or an ant!

On Your Head

Look around. You see children with black hair. Others have brown or blond hair. A few have red hair.

These kids have different hair colors.

Hair color is a trait. Genes give directions for hair color.

This girl has brown hair. Brown hair is a trait.

How do genes control hair color? They tell the body to make certain pigments. Pigments color hair. Genes also tell the body how much pigment to make.

Pigment is a substance that gives color to something. Your skin has pigment too.

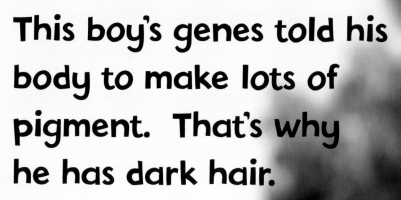

This boy's genes told his body to make lots of pigment. That's why he has dark hair.

A gene comes in two different forms, called alleles. This boy has alleles for dark hair.

This girl's genes told her body to make less pigment. That's why she has light hair.

This girl has alleles for light hair.

Redheads

Do you know anyone with red hair? Fewer people have red hair than any other color.

This boy has red hair. It is not a common hair color.

Red hair comes from a special pigment. One allele of a gene tells the body to make it. A person needs two copies of this allele to have red hair.

These kids got an allele for red hair from their mom. They also got one from their dad. That's why they have red hair!

Everyone in this family has genes for red hair!

These parents have brown hair. But one of their children has red hair. **How can that happen?** Each parent has one allele for red hair. One daughter has two copies of that allele. She got one from each parent.

Curly or Straight

You might have straight hair.

Your friend's hair might be wavy.

18

Another friend might have tightly curled hair. Genes tell your body to grow straight, wavy, or curly hair.

For many traits, one of a pair of genes takes control. But that's not true for hair texture.

Some members of this family have straight hair. Others have curly hair.

20

Different directions from many genes blend together.

These sports fans have all different kinds of hair textures. Some hair is wavy, some is curly, and some is straight.

The girl on the right got alleles for straight hair from her dad. She got alleles for curly hair from her mom. Her hair is wavy. It is curlier than her dad's hair. But it is less curly than her mom's.

This girl has wavy hair.

Uncommon Traits

Some hair traits are less common than color or curls. This man has a patch of white hair above his forehead. The trait is called a white forelock.

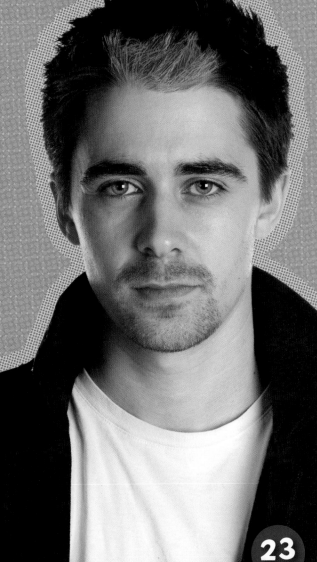

A child needs only one allele for a white forelock to have one. Often members of a family share this trait.

Pull back the hair on your forehead. Do you see a V-shaped point? This trait is called a widow's peak.

This is a widow's peak.

This boy has a widow's peak but this girl does not. Her hairline is straight. Scientists aren't sure how genes control widow's peaks.

Hair can be straight or curly. It can be black, brown, blond, or red. What hair traits do you have?

Activity
Track the Traits!

Track the different hair traits in your classroom. List these traits on a sheet of lined paper:

black hair   curly hair   widow's peak
brown hair   wavy hair   no widow's peak
blond hair   straight hair
red hair

Then divide your paper into two columns. One column will be for the traits. The other column will be for tally marks. (You'll find out what tally marks are and how to use them next.) Your paper should look like the sample sheet on page 29 when you're done.

Put a tally mark next to each trait that you have. A tally mark is a straight up-and-down line, like this:

|

Then ask your classmates about their hair traits. Make a tally mark for all your classmates next to their hair traits. When you get to five, put a diagonal line through your tally marks, like this:

That's how you write the number five in tally marks.
For the number six, make a new tally mark, like this:

When you're done tallying the hair traits, count how many
of you have each trait. Which trait got the most tallies?

Sample Sheet:

Hair Traits	Tally Marks
black hair	
brown hair	
blond hair	
red hair	
curly hair	
wavy hair	
straight hair	
widow's peak	
no widow's peak	

Glossary

allele: one of two or more forms of a gene

birth parent: a parent who is genetically related to his or her child

gene: one of the parts of the cells of all living things. Genes are passed from parents to children and determine how you look and the way you grow.

pigment: a substance that gives color to something

trait: a quality or characteristic that makes one person or thing different from another

white forelock: a patch of white hair above the forehead

widow's peak: a V-shaped point formed by hair in the middle of the forehead

Further Reading

Dragonfly TV: Dog Breeding
http://pbskids.org/dragonflytv/
games/game_dogbreeding.html

Harris, Trudy. *Tally Cat Keeps Track.* Minneapolis:
Millbrook Press, 2011.

KidsHealth: What Is a Gene?
http://kidshealth.org/kid/talk/qa/what_is_gene.html

OLogy: The Gene Scene
http://www.amnh.org/ology/genetics

Silverman, Buffy. *Body Parts: Double-Jointedness,
Hitchhiker's Thumb, and More.* Minneapolis: Lerner
Publications Company, 2013.

Simpson, Kathleen. *Genetics: From DNA
to Designer Dogs.* Washington, DC:
National Geographic,
2008.

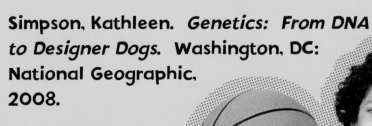

Index

Photo Acknowledgments

The images in this book are used with the permission of: © Allenfive5/Dreamstime. com, p. 1; © Tom Merton/OJO Images/Getty Images, p. 2; © Lindas131/Dreamstime.com, p. 4; © Sonya Farrell/Photodisc/Getty Images, p. 5; © Comstock Images/Getty Images, p. 6; © Lilly Dong/Botanica/Getty Images, p. 7; © Shalom Ormbsy/Blend Images/ CORBIS, p. 8; © Altrendo Images/Stockbyte/Getty Images, p. 9; © Allana Wesley White/CORBIS, p. 10; © Monkeybusinessimages/Dreamstime.com, p. 11; © Get4net/ Dreamstime.com, p. 12; © David Madison/The Image Bank/Getty Images, p. 13; © Radius Images/Getty Images, p. 14; © Daniel MacDonald/www.dmacphoto.com/Flickr/Getty Images, p. 15; © Radius Images/Getty Images, p. 16; © Eric Audras/Getty Images, p. 17; © Ryan McVay/Stone/Getty Images, p. 18; © Image Source/Getty Images, p. 19; © Mango Prodcutions/CORBIS, p. 20; © Chris Whitehead/Cultura/Getty Images, p. 21; © Sean De Burca/CORBIS, p. 22; © JmPaget/Dreamstime.com, p. 23; © Wavebreakmedia Ltd/Dreamstime.com, p. 24; © Brand X Pictures/Getty Images, p. 25; © Design Pics/Colleen Cahill/Getty Images, p. 26 (left); © Xalanx/Dreamstime. com, p. 26 (right); © Jupiterimages/Brand X Pictures/Getty Images, p. 27; © Anna Emilia/Getty Images, p. 30; © Michael Mahovlich/First Light/Getty Images, p. 31.

Front cover: © Godfer/Dreamstime.com.

Main body text set in Johann Light 30/36.